Contents

Part One: Pensions

Part Two: Finances After Retirement

Introduction

Enjoying a fruitful and prosperous retirement is the goal of most people, yet when the day finally arrives quite often the finances necessary to ensure a peaceful old age are just not there. There are many reasons for this, the most common being lack of adequate planning in the earlier, more productive years. In addition, lack of knowledge of exactly what is on offer for those who have reached retirement age, such as the range of benefits available, along with other age related benefits also contributes to the relative poverty of today's retirees.

The aim of this book is to explain, in as much depth as possible, the workings of the pension industry, how you can maximise your pension before retiring, and also how to take care of other fundamental areas of life such as planning for care and maintaining good health.

The emphasis of this book is, as the title states, on the planning and management of finances following retirement, and ensuring that all areas of life which require financial know how and management are explored. The book covers pensions, continuing to work, taxation, health and care and also the management of your home.

We all want to enjoy our retirement in peace and be relatively prosperous. It is hoped that this book will at least provide a stepping-stone to this end.

Patrick Grant

1

Pensions Generally

Planning for the future

The main principle with all pension provision is that the sooner you start saving money in a pension plan the more that you will have at retirement. The later that you leave it the less you will have or the more expensive that it will be to create a fund adequate enough for your needs.

In order to gauge your retirement needs, you will need to have a clear idea of your lifestyle, or potential lifestyle in retirement. This is not something that you can plan, or want to plan, at a younger age but the main factor is that the more that you have the easier life will be. There are two main factors which currently underpin retirement:

- Improved health and longevity-we are living longer and we have better health so therefore we are more active
- People are better off-improved state and company pensions

Sources of pension and other retirement income

Government statistics indicate that there is a huge gap between the poorest and richest pensioners in the United Kingdom. No surprise there. The difference between the two groups is about £700 per week. The poorest fifth of pensioners in the UK are reliant mainly on state benefits whilst the wealthier groups have occupational incomes and also personal investment incomes. The table below indicates the disparity between different socio-economic groups:

TYPE OF PENSIONER HOUSEHOLD

SINGLE   COUPLE

	Poorest Fifth	Middle Fifth	Wealthiest fifth	P Fifth	M Fifth	W Fifth
BEFORE TAX WEEKLY INCOME OF WHICH:	£100	£169	£392	£170	£292	£855
STATE PENSIONS	£90	£133	£141	£145	£188	£162
OCCUPATIONAL PENSIONS	£5	£26	£138	£15	£71	£306
PERSONAL PENSION	£1	£2	£11	£4	£8	£41
INVESTMENT INCOME	£3	£5	£49	£4	£11	£146
EARNINGS	£0	£2	£$5	£2	£12	£183
OTHER INCOME	£1	£1	£7	£1	£1	£15

SOURCE: The Pensioners Income Series 2006-2007.

The above graphically illustrates that those in the middle and wealthiest bands have, through one means or another, managed to ensure that there is enough money in the pot to cater for retirement. Those in the lower income bands rely almost exclusively on state pensions and other benefits.

When attempting to forecast for future pension needs, there are a number of factors which need to be taken into account:

- Your income needs in retirement and how much of that income you can expect to derive from state pensions
- How much pension that any savings you have will produce
- How long you have to save for
- Projected inflation

1. Income needs in retirement

This is very much a personal decision and will be influenced by a number of factors, such as ongoing housing costs, care costs, projected lifestyle etc. The main factor is that you have enough to live on comfortably. In retirement you will probably take more holidays and want to enjoy your free time. This costs money so your future planning should take into account all your projected needs and costs. The next chapter includes a few calculations about future needs. When calculating future needs, all sources of income should be taken into account.

2. What period to save over

The obvious fact is that, the longer period that you save over the more you will build up and hence the more that you will have in retirement. As time goes on savings are compounded and the value of the pot goes up. One thing is for certain and that is if you leave it too late then you will have to put away a large slice of your income to produce a decent pension. If you plan to retire at an early age then you will need to save more to produce the same benefits.

3. Inflation

As prices rise, so your money buys you less. This is the main effect of inflation and to maintain the same level of spending power you will need to save more as time goes on. Many forms of retirement plans will include a calculation for inflation. Currently, inflation is at a reasonable level, 1.1% (November 2009) per annum. However, history shows that the effects of inflation can be corrosive, having risen above 25% per annum in the past. Hopefully, this is now under control

****

2

How Much Income Do You Need in Retirement?

Many people need far less in retirement than when actively working. The expenses that exist when working, such as mortgage payments, children and work related expenses do not (usually) exist when retired. The average household between 30-49 spends £473 per week and £416 between 50-64. This drops to £263 per week between 65 to 74 and even lower in later retirement (Family Expenditure Survey 2000-1).

However, as might be expected, expenditure on health care increases correspondingly with age. Whilst the state may help with some costs the individual still has to bear a high proportion of expenditure on health related items.

When calculating how much money you will need in retirement, it is useful to use a table in order to list your anticipated expenses as follows:

1. Everyday needs

Item	Annual Total £
Food and other	
Leisure (newspapers etc)	

Pets	
Clothes	
Other household items	
Gardening	
General expenses	

Home expenses

Mortgage/rent	
Service charges/repairs	
Insurance	
Council tax	
Water and other utilities	
Telephone	
TV licence other charges (satellite)	
Other expenses (home help)	

Leisure and general entertainment

Hobbies	
Eating out	
Cinema/theatre	
Holidays	
Other luxuries (smoking/drinking	

Transport

Car expenses	

Car hire	
Petrol etc	
Bus/train fares	

Health

Dental charges	
Optical expenses	
Medical insurance	
Care insurance	
Other health related expenses	

Anniversaries/birthdays etc

Children/grandchildren	
Relatives other than children	
Christmas	
Charitable donations	
Other expenses	

Savings and loans

General savings	
Saving for later retirement	
Other savings	
Loan repayments	

Other

3

Sources Of Pension

The state pension

The state pension system is based on contributions, the payments made by an individual today funds tomorrow's pension payments. Therefore, the state pension system is not a savings scheme it is a pay-as-you-go system.

Pensions are a major area of government spending and are becoming more and more so. Protecting pensions against inflationary increases have put pressure on respective governments, along with the introduction of a second tier-pension, the state second pension (S2P). This replaced SERPS. The problems of pension provision are set to increase with the numbers of older people outnumbering those in active work, leading to an imbalance in provision. The biggest dilemma facing the government, and future governments, is the problem of convincing people to save for their pensions, therefore taking some of the burden off the state.

Those most at risk in terms of retirement poverty are the lower earners, who quite often do not build up enough contributions to gain a state pension, those who contribute to a state pension but cannot save enough to contribute to a private scheme and disabled people who cannot work or carers who also cannot work. The above is not an exclusive list. The government has recognised the difficulties faced by these groups and have introduced the state second pension and pension credits.

Pension credits

Pension credits began life in October 2003. The credit is designed to top up the resources of pensioners whose income is low. The pension credit has two components: a guarantee credit and a saving credit. The guarantee credit is available to anyone over 60 years of age whose income is less than a set amount called the minimum guarantee. The guarantee will bring income up to £124.05 for a single person and £189.35 for a couple (including same sex couples) (2009-2010). The minimum guarantee is higher for certain categories of disabled people and carers.

The savings credit

Pension credit also has an inbuilt incentive scheme called a savings credit which encourages people to save for their retirement.

The rules are complicated. If a person is aged 65 or over they can claim a credit of 60pence for each £1 of income that they have between two thresholds. The lower threshold is the maximum basic state pension. The upper threshold is the minimum guarantee stated above (£130 single and £198.45 couple 2009/10). This gives a maximum savings threshold of £20.40 single and £27.03 couple (2009/10). Savings credit is reduced by 40p for each £1 of income above the minimum guarantee.

The over 80 pension

This is a non-contributory pension for people aged 80 or over with little or no state pension. If you are 80 or over, not getting or getting a reduced state pension because you have not paid enough National Insurance contributions (NI) and are currently living in England, Scotland or Wales and have been doing so for a total of 10 years or more in any continuous period of 20 years before or after your 80th birthday, you could claim the over 80 pension. The maximum amount of the over 80 state pension that you can get is 60% of the full state pension.

****

4

The State Pension

Over 96% of single pensioners and 99% of couples receive the Basic state pension. Therefore, it is here to stay. Everyone who has paid the appropriate national insurance contributions will be entitled to a state pension. If you are not working you can either receive pension credits, as discussed, or make voluntary contributions.

The basic state pension is paid at a flat rate, currently single person £92.25 per week, married £190.50 (2009/10). A married couple can qualify for a higher pension based on the husband's NI contributions. If the wife has reached pension age her part of the pension is paid directly to her. If the wife is below pension age, the whole pension is paid directly to the husband.

If both members of a couple qualify for a full pension based on their contributions then together they will receive twice the single amount.

Basic state pensions are increased each April in line with price inflation. State pensioners also receive a (£10 Christmas bonus-check current entitlement) and are entitled to winter fuel payments.

At the moment, only married women can claim a pension based on their spouse's NI record. This is set to change and married men who have reached 65 will be able to claim a basic state pension based on their wife's contribution record where the wife reaches state pension age on or after 6th April 2010.

Same sex couples, as a result of the Civil Partnerships Act 2004, have the same rights as heterosexual couples in all aspects of pension provision.

Qualifying for state pension

In order to receive the full basic pension, if you reach state pension age before 6th April 2010 the main rule is that you will have to have paid NI contributions for at least 90% of the tax years in your working life. If you have only paid for a quarter, for example, you may not get basic state pension. 'Working life' is defined as from the age 16 to retirement age, or the last complete tax year before retirement age. For men and women born after 5th March 1955 the working life is 49 years. For women with a pension age of 60, the working life is 44 years. The table overleaf indicates likely pension related to NI contributions. If you reach state pension age after 6th April 2010 then you will need 30 qualifying years in order to get the full state pension

State pensions related to NI contributions
Number of years for % of full basic pension which you have made contributions for, for which you qualify.

See overleaf.

NI contributions

Women born after 5 March 1955 and all men		Women born on or Before April 5 1950
9 or less	0	0
10	26	0
11	29	25
12	31	28
13	34	30
14	36	32
15	39	35
16	42	37
17	44	39
18	47	41
19	49	44
20	52	46
21	54	48
22	57	50
23	59	53
24	62	55
25	65	57
26	67	60
27	70	62
28	72	64
29	75	66
30	77	69

31	80	71
32	83	73
33	85	75
34	88	78
35	90	80
36	93	82
37	95	85
38	98	87
39	100	89
40	100	91
41	100	94
42	100	96
43	100	98
44 or over	100	100

For NI contributions to count towards a state pension, they must be the right type, as the table below indicates.

NI contributions counting towards a basic state pension.

Type of contribution   Description   Right type?

Type of contribution	Description	Right type?
Class 1 full rate	Paid by employees and their employers including company directors but not paid if earnings are below a set limit	YES
Class 1, reduced	Paid by some	NO

rate	married women and widows	
Class 2	Paid by self employed people. Optional if profits are below a set level. Optional for some married women and widows	YES
Class 3	Voluntary	YES
Class 4	Paid by self employed people with profits below set levels	NO

If you earn less than what is known as the 'primary threshold' (£110 per week in 2009-10) you do not pay national insurance contributions. However, the year will still count towards building up your basic state pension provided that you earn at least the lower earnings limit (LEL). In 2009-2010 this is £95 per week.

Class 1 contributions

Class 1 contributions are paid if earnings are above the primary threshold. The Threshold, set by government annually, is currently £110 per week (tax year 2009/10). If your earnings are above this set limit then you will be paying contributions at class 1 that build up to a state pension.

The level of contribution is set at 11% of earnings above the primary threshold level up to an upper earnings limit which is £844 per week in 2009/10. Contributions are paid at 1% of earnings above the upper earnings limit. If a person earns less than the primary threshold they will not pay NI contributions. The year will still count towards building up a basic state pension provided the earnings are not less than the lower earnings limit. This is £95 at 2009/10.

Class 2 contributions

Self-employed people will build up their NI contributions by paying class 2 contributions. These are paid either by direct debit or by quarterly bill at the rate of £2.40 per week (2009/10).

If profits are below the 'small earnings exception' which is £5075 in 2009/10 then there is a choice of whether or not to pay NI contributions. However, if this option is chosen, then a state pension will not be building up and there could be a loss of other benefits, such as sickness, bereavement and incapacity.

If you are a director of your own company then class 1 contributions will be paid and not class 2.

NI contribution credits

If a person is not working, in some cases they will be credited with NI contributions. This applies in the following circumstances:

- If claiming certain state benefits such as jobseekers allowance, maternity allowance or incapacity benefit
- To men and women under state pension age who have reached 60 but stopped work
- For the years in which a person has had their 16th, 17th or 18th birthday if they were still at school and were born after 5th April 1957.

If a person stays at home in order to look after children or a sick or elderly relative they might qualify for Home Responsibilities Protection. This reduces the number of years of NI contributions that are needed to qualify for a given level of pension. People who are not working and are claiming child benefit will receive Home Responsibilities Protection automatically.

Class 3 contributions

If a person is not paying class 1 or 2 contributions or receiving HRP they can pay class 3 voluntary contributions. These are charged at a flat rate of £12.05 per week (2009/10). They can be paid up to 6 years back to make up any shortfall.

State pensions for people over 80

From the age of 80, all pensioners qualify for an extra 25pence per week If a person does not qualify for a basic state pension or is on a low income then they may be entitled to receive what is called ' an over-80's pension' from the age of 80.

For further advice concerning pensions either go to the government website www.thepensionsservice.gov.uk or refer to the list of useful leaflets at the back of this book.

Additional state pension

S2P replaced the State Earnings Related Pension (SERPS) in April 2002. SERPS was, essentially, a state second tier pension and it was compulsory to pay into this in order to supplement the basic state pension. There were drawbacks however, and many people fell through the net so S2P was introduced to allow other groups to contribute. S2P refined SERPS allowing the following to contribute:

- people caring for children under six and entitled to child benefit
- carers looking after someone who is elderly or disabled, if they are entitled to carers allowance
- certain people who are unable to work because of illness or disability, if they are entitled to long-term incapacity benefit or severe disablement allowance and they have been in the workforce for at least one-tenth of their working life

Self-employed people are excluded from S2P as are employees earning less than the lower earnings limit. Married women and widows paying class 1 contributions at the reduced rate do not build up additional state pension. S2P is an earnings related scheme. This means that people on high earnings build up more pension than those on lower earnings. However, people earning at least the lower earnings limit (£95) in 2009/10 but less than the low earnings threshold (£110) in 2009/10 are treated as if they have earnings at that level and so build up more pension than they otherwise would.

Contracting out

A person does not build up state additional pension during periods when they are contracted out. Contracting out means that a person has opted to join an occupational scheme or a personal pensions scheme or stakeholder pension. While contacted out, a person will pay lower National Insurance Contributions on part of earnings or some of the contributions paid by an employee and employer are 'rebated' and paid into the occupational pension scheme or other pension scheme.

****

5

Job Related Pensions

The best way to save for retirement is through an occupational pension scheme. Employers will also contribute and pay administration costs. Schemes normally provide an additional package of benefits such as protection if you become disabled, protection for dependants and protection against inflation.

Some pension schemes are related to final salary and provide a pension that equates to a proportion of salary. However, it must be said that a lot of these schemes are winding down.

Limits on your pension savings

These limits apply collectively to all private pensions (occupational schemes and personal pensions) that you may have)

See overleaf

Type of limit	Description	Amount
Annual contribution limit	The maximum contributions on which you can get tax relief. You can continue contributing to your 75th birthday	£3,600 or 100% of your UK relevant earnings for the year whichever is the greater
Annual allowance	The maximum addition to your pension savings in any one year (including for example employers contributions). Anything above the limit normally triggers a tax charge, but this does not apply in the year that you start to draw the pension.	Tax year 2009/10 £245,000
Lifetime allowance	The cumulative value of benefits that can be drawn from your pension savings. Any amount drawn that exceeds the limits triggers a tax charge.	Tax year 2009/10 £1.75 Million

Tax advantages of occupational schemes

The tax advantages of occupational schemes are:

- a person receives tax relief on the amount that he or she pays into the scheme
- employers contributions count as a tax-free benefit
- capital gains on the contributions build up tax free
- at retirement part of the pension fund can be taken as a tax-free lump sum. The rest is taken as a taxable pension

People aged 65 and over receive more generous tax allowances than younger people. Tax allowances are dealt with further on in the book.

Qualifying to join an occupational scheme

An occupational scheme can be either open to all or restricted to certain groups, i.e. different schemes for different groups. Schemes are not allowed to discriminate in terms of race or gender or any other criteria. Employees do not have to join a scheme and can leave when they wish. There might however be restrictions on rejoining or joining a scheme later on.

Not all employers offer an occupational scheme. Another pension arrangement such as a stakeholder scheme or Group Pension Scheme might be offered. However, following the passage of the 2008 Pensions Act it will be compulsory, by 2010 for all employers to offer access to a personal pension scheme.

The amount of pension that a person receives from an occupational scheme will depend in part on the type of scheme that it is. Currently, there are two main types:

- defined benefit schemes, promising a given level of benefit on retirement, usually final salary schemes
- money purchase schemes (defined contribution schemes), where a person builds up their own savings pot. There are hybrid schemes where both the above are on offer but these are not common.

Final salary schemes

With final salary schemes, a person is promised (but not guaranteed) a certain level of pension and other benefits related to earnings. This is independent of what is paid into the scheme. Final salary schemes work well when a person stays with their employer for a long length of time or work in the public sector.

A person in such a scheme will typically pay around 5% of their salary into the scheme with the employer paying the balance of the cost which will be around 10% of salary on average. When the stock market is doing well the employer is safeguarded but when the economic climate is changing, such as at this point in time then the story is somewhat different and the employer has to pay more to maintain the level of pension. This is why such pension schemes are being withdrawn. The pension received at retirement is based on a formula and related to final salary and years of membership in the scheme. The maximum usually builds up over 40 years. The accrual rate in such a scheme is one sixtieth or one eightieth of salary per year in the scheme.

If a person leaves the pension scheme before retirement they are still entitled to receive a pension from the scheme, based on contributions.

'Final salary' defined

The final salary is defined in the rules of the scheme. It can have a variety of meanings, for example average pay over a number of years, average of the best salary for a number of years out of ten, or earnings on a specified date. What counts are the pensionable earnings, which may mean basic salary, or could include other elements such as overtime, bonus etc.

A lump sum tax-free is included in the scheme which is defined by Inland Revenue rules. The lump sum after 40 years of service will be around 1.5 times the annual salary.

Money purchase schemes

Money purchase pension schemes are like any other forms of savings or investment. Money is paid in and grows in value and the proceeds eventually provide a pension. The scheme is straightforward and has its upsides and downsides. The upside is that it is simple and portable. The downside is that it is related to the growth of the economy and can shrink as well as grow. It is more difficult to plan for retirement with this kind of scheme, as distinct from the final salary scheme. As we have seen, employers prefer this kind of scheme because, although they pay into it, it doesn't place any onerous responsibilities on them.

The pension that is received on retirement will depend on the amount paid into the scheme, charges deducted for management of the scheme, how well the investment grows and the rate, called the annuity rate, at which the fund can be converted into pension. A major problem for pension schemes has been the decline in annuity rates in recent years.

With most money purchase schemes the proceeds are usually given to an insurer who will administer the funds. The trustees of the scheme will choose the insurer, in most cases. In some cases, contributors are given the choice of investment. This choice will usually include:

- a with-profits basis which is a medium-risk option and which is safer and more likely to provide a good return if a person remains with the same employer. The value of the fund cannot fall and will grow steadily as reversionary bonuses are added. On retirement a person will receive a terminal bonus, which represents a chunk of the overall return
- a unit linked fund- where money is invested in one or more funds, e.g. shares, property, gilts and so on.

The cash balance scheme

A cash balance scheme lies somewhere between a final salary scheme and a money purchase scheme. Whereas in a final salary scheme a person is promised a certain level of pension at retirement with a cash balance scheme a person is promised a certain amount of money with which to buy a pension. The amount of cash can be expressed in a number of ways, for example as a percentage of salary per annum for each year of membership. So if a person is earning £50,000 per annum and the cash balance scheme is promising 15% of salary for each year of membership, there would be a pension fund of £50,000 times 15% which equals £75,000 after 10 years of membership.

****

6

Personal Pension Arrangements

Occupational pensions

We discuss occupational pension schemes in more depth later in this book. Briefly, occupational pension schemes are a very important source of income. They are also one of the best ways to pay into a pension scheme as the employer has to contribute a significant amount to the pot. Over the years the amounts paid into occupational pension schemes have increased significantly. Although there have been a number of incidences of occupational schemes being wound up this is relatively small and they remain a key source of retirement income.

Stakeholder schemes

Stakeholder pension schemes are designed for those people who do not have an employer, or have an employer who does not have an occupational scheme. They therefore cannot pay into an occupational scheme. If an employer does not offer an occupational scheme (many small employers are exempt) they have to arrange access to a stakeholder scheme. Employees do not have to join an occupational scheme offered by employers, instead they can join a stakeholder scheme. Likewise, self-employed people can also join a stakeholder scheme.

Stakeholder schemes have a contribution limit-this being currently £3,600 per year. Anyone who is not earning can also pay into a scheme, up to the limit above. A stakeholder pension is one form of personal pension described below.

The range of personal pensions

Personal pensions are open to anyone, in much the same way as a stakeholder scheme. These are described more fully later on in this book. Employers do not have to offer a personal pension scheme through the workplace, as they do a stakeholder scheme, though a lot do by offering a group scheme which has been separately negotiated with a provider.

Other ways to save for retirement

The government offers certain tax advantages to encourage pension saving. However, the most advantageous savings plan is the Individual Savings Account (ISA) discussed further on in the book.

****

7

Changes to Private Pension Savings

In 2006, important changes were introduced to the way people save for their pensions. The cumulative changes over the years meant that the whole pension system had become very complex and some streamlining was needed.

The lifetime allowance

From 2006, there is a single lifetime limit on the amount of savings that a person can build up through various pension schemes and plans that are subject to tax relief. The lifetime allowance starts at £1.75 million in the current tax year 2009/10 and will be increased each year. The increases will be aimed at keeping the lifetime limit in line with inflation.

The lifetime allowance applies to savings in all types of pension schemes including occupational pensions and stakeholder schemes. There are, broadly, two types of scheme or plan:

- Defined contribution-with these types of schemes money goes in and is invested with the fund used to buy a pension. Basically, if the fund at retirement is £200,000 then £200,000 lifetime allowance has been used up

- Defined benefit-in this type of scheme, a person is promised a pension of a certain amount usually worked out on the basis of salary before retirement and the length of time that you have been in the scheme. The equation for working out lifetime benefit in this type of scheme is a little more complicated. The pension is first converted into a notional sum (the amount of money it is reckoned is needed to buy a pension of that size). The government sets out a factor that it says will be needed to make the conversion which it has said is 20. If the pension is £20,000 then this is calculated as 20,000 times 20,000 which is £400,000. Therefore £400,000 will be used up from the lifetime allowance.

If a person has already started to take some pension before April 6th 2006, this will be treated as using up a percentage of the lifetime allowance. The pension already started will be multiplied by a factor of 25 to find the amount of lifetime allowance used up. For example, if you are receiving £3,600 per annum this will be multiplied by 25 which means that £90,000 will be deducted from your lifetime allowance for 2009/10.

The annual allowance

In addition to the lifetime allowance, there will be an annual allowance starting at £245,000 in 2009/10. This is the amount that pension savings may increase each year whether through contributions paid in or to promised benefits. An addition to the promised benefits must be converted to a notional lump sum before it can be compared with the annual allowance. The government has stated that a factor of 10 should be used as a multiplier. For example, if a promised pension increases by £300, this is equivalent to a lump sum of 10 times £300 = £3,000, therefore using up £3000 of the annual allowance. The limit will be revised each year and can be obtained from the government pensions website www.thepensionsservice.gov.uk.

The annual allowance will not start in the year a person starts their pension or die. This gives a person scope to make large last-minute additions to their fund.

If at retirement the value of a pension exceeds the lifetime allowance there will be an income tax charge of 55% on the excess if it is taken as a lump sum, or 25% if it is left in the scheme to be taken as a pension, which is taxable as income.

If the increase in the value of savings in any year exceeds the annual allowance, the excess is taxed at 40%.

Limits to benefits and contributions

The present benefit and contribution limits have been scrapped. The only remaining restrictions are:

- Contributions-the maximum that can be paid in each year is either the amount equal to taxable earnings or £3,600 whichever is the greater
- Tax free lump sum-at retirement a person can take up to one quarter of the value of the total pension fund as a tax free lump sum

In the case of death before retirement, in general savings can be paid out to survivors either as an income or as a lump sum. A lump sum up to the value of the lifetime limit will be tax-free but anything over will be taxed at 55%.

If a person leaves a scheme before two years membership they can take a refund of contributions. Refunds are paid after deduction of tax at 20% on the first £10,800 and 40% on any excess.

Tax relief on contributions will either be given at source or through PAYE if relevant.

Taking a pension

With the exception of ill-health, a person must start their pension at a minimum age, currently 50 but due to rise to 55 by 2010 and maximum age 75. Schemes will administer the rules for retirement in the minimum age to 55. Special rules will safeguard the rights of people in certain occupations to retire earlier provided they had this right already on 10th December 2003, but the lifetime limit will be reduced where it is to be applied at an earlier age. The reduction will be 2.5% of the limit for every year in advance of age 55. Any unused part of the lifetime allowance can be carried forward to set against future pension earnings.

Savings do not have to be converted into pension in one go. This can be staggered and pension income can be increased as a person winds down from work.

For each tranche of pension started before 75, there is a range of choices. This will depend on the rules of each individual scheme. A person can:

- have a pension paid direct from an occupational pension scheme
- use a pension fund to purchase an annuity to provide a pension for the rest of life
- use part of the pension to buy a limited period annuity lasting just five years leaving the rest invested
- opt for income drawdown which allows taking of a pension whilst leaving the rest invested. The tax-free lump sum could be taken and the rest left invested. The maximum income will be 120% of a standard annuity rate published by the Financial Services Authority. On death the remaining pension fund can be used to provide pensions for dependants or paid to survivors as a lump sum, taxed at 35%.

When a person reaches 75 years of age, they must opt for one of the following choices:

- have a pension paid direct from an occupational scheme
- use the pension fund to buy an annuity to provide a pension for the rest of life or
- opt for an Alternatively Secured Pension or ASP. This is pension draw down but with the maximum income limited to 70% of the annuity rate for a 75 year old. the minimum income is nil. On death, the remaining fund can be used to provide dependants pensions or, if there

are no dependants, left to a charity or absorbed into the scheme to help other people's pensions. The person(s) whose pensions are to be enhanced can be nominated by the person whose pension it is.

****

8

Increasing a Pension

State pension

There are a number of ways that a person may be able to increase the pension that you get from the state. If the Retirement Pension Forecast that is sent out by the Department for Work and Pensions shows that a reduced state pension is due, it may be possible to increase the amount that is received by paying voluntary Class 3 National Insurance contributions. It is possible to go back six-years to fill any gaps in a NI record.

If you go back two years, you pay contributions that applied in the earlier year. If you go back further, you will pay the rate for the year when the payment is made.

Married women's reduced rate contributions.

If a women is paying National Insurance at the married women's reduced rate, they may want to consider switching to full rate contributions instead, which will result in an increased pension. For older women, the switch to full-rate contributions generates very little extra pension. A local taxation office can advise appropriately. Leaflet CA13 National

Insurance for Married Women gives details on how to make the switch.

Delaying retirement

The state pension age is currently 65 for men and 60 for women. A person can defer the date of retirement and so increase their entitlement. The whole pension must be deferred and the whole pension will benefit from the increase. Any pension for a wife based on husbands contributions must also be deferred if the husband makes this choice.

At present, it is possible to defer a pension for five years. The eventual pension will be increased by 7.5% per year if deferred. It is possible to take the increase as a lump sum, if the pension is deferred for at least a year. The amount of lump sum depends on the interest rate used by the government. The lump sum is taxable.

Occupational pension schemes

HMRC rules allow a person to pay up to £245,000 of their earnings into a pension fund (2009/10). In practice, most people pay far less than this. This can be achieved by paying Additional Voluntary Contributions (AVC's).

As with ordinary contributions, a person qualifies for tax-relief at the top rate of tax on the amount that is paid in AVC's. Capital gains from investing the AVC's are tax free. Part of the investment income is tax free but not income from shares, unit trusts or similar investments.

An employer who operates an in-house occupational scheme must also offer an in-house AVC scheme to enable members to make extra contributions. This scheme will normally work on a money purchase basis and money will be invested to top-up the occupational scheme. Some in-house schemes, mainly public sector schemes offer an added years AVC scheme. This is available when the main pension works on a final salary, or similar basis. Added years can be purchased from the main scheme and credited to the account of the pension holder. Another option is to pay into an independent AVC scheme offered by insurance companies and pension providers.

Personal pensions

A person can maximise the amount that they are allowed to save by making careful use of the basis-year rules. These let a person base the contributions made now on the level of earnings from any of the last five years. The year with the highest level of earnings should be chosen as the basis-year.

If a person has a retirement annuity contract there is another way to catch up on retirement savings if the full contributions limit hasn't been used up in the past few years. The carry forward rules can be used to carry forward any unused contributions relief from the last six-years. The carry forward is from the earliest tax-year first.

Combining carry-forward and carry-back rules

Carry-back and carry-forward rules can be combined, which means that a person can get unused relief from seven years ago.

For example, if a contribution is made in 2008/9 it can be carried back and treated as if it was paid in 2007/8. The carry back can then be from 2000/1.

Combining carry-back and carry-forward rules can be a good idea:

- if there is a large chunk of unused tax relief in the year seven years back. If not used now it will be lost
- tax rates are lower in the current year than in the previous year and a person wants to maximise relief on large contributions
- a persons marginal rate of tax was higher in the earlier years and there is a wish to maximise relief on over-large contributions.

Personal pensions and retirement annuity contracts

A person with a retirement annuity contract can choose to make contributions to the contract, a personal pension plan or both. The choice that is made each year will affect the amount of carry-forward relief available for the retirement annuity contract.

****

9

Tax and Pensions

State pensions

State retirement pensions count as income for tax purposes. Tax may have to be paid if income received is high enough. The only exception to this is the £10 Christmas bonus paid to all pensioners.

State pension is paid without deduction of tax. This is convenient for non-taxpayers. For other taxpayers, the tax due will usually be deducted from PAYE or from any other pension that is received. If the tax is not deducted it will be collected through self-assessment in January and July instalments.

Occupational schemes

A pension from an occupational scheme is treated as income for tax purposes. Usually, the pension will be paid with tax deducted through the PAYE system, along with any other tax due.

Personal pensions

A personal pension will count as income for tax purposes. The pension provider will usually deduct tax through PAYE.

Likewise, any other tax due will be deducted through the PAYE system. The local tax office should be contacted in order to determine individual tax positions.

Tax in retirement

When a person retires, their tax bill continues to be worked out in the usual way. However, higher tax allowances may apply so less tax is paid. The calculations used to work out a person's individual tax bill are as follows:

- income from all sources is added together. This includes all income with the exception of income that is tax-free.
- outgoings that you pay in full are deducted from taxable income. 'Outgoings' means any expenditure that qualifies for tax relief.
- allowances are subtracted. Everyone has a personal allowance. For current allowances, contact the local HMRC Office or Citizens Advice Bureau. There is a breakdown below
- What is left is taxable income. This divided into three. The first slice 10% is paid (£2090) the second slice tax is paid at the basic rate (£32,400) the third slice is subject to 40% tax.
- Married couples allowance-this is a reduced rate allowance, given at a rate of 10% as a reduction to a person's tax bill. Married couples allowance is given only where a husband or wife were born before 6th April 1935.

Tax allowances for retirees

In the tax year 2009/10 the basic personal allowance for most people is £6475. However, if a person is 65 or over at any time during a tax year, there will be a higher personal allowance, the age-allowance. There are two rates of age allowance: in the 2009/10 tax year the allowance is £9490   for people reaching ages 65 to 74, and the higher age allowance is £9640 for people reaching ages 75 or more. A husband and wife can each get a personal allowance to set against their own income. There is an extra allowance called a married couples allowance if either husband or wife, or both, were born before 6th April 1935. In 2008/9 this is £6535 if the older partner is aged up to 73 at the start of the tax year and £6625 if the older partner is aged 74 or over. However, for the tax year 2009/10 this is non-applicable.

While the personal allowance saves tax at the highest rate, the married couples allowance only gives tax relief at the rate of 10% in the 2009/10tax year. If the husbands income is above a certain level then the married couples allowance is reduced, but never to less than a basic amount. A wife can elect to have half the basic amount of the married couples allowance (but not any of the age-related addition) set against her own income. Alternatively, the husband and wife can elect jointly for the whole basic amount to be transferred to the wife.

Income limit for age allowance

Age allowances are reduced for people with earnings above a certain level. The personal age allowance is reduced if a person has a total income of more than £21,800 in the tax year 2008/9. The married couple's age allowance is also reduced if this is the case. In either case, the reduction is £1 for every £2 over the limit.

Where the husband is receiving both age-related personal allowance and age-related married couple's allowance, his personal allowance is reduced first and then the married couple's allowance. The reduction stops once the allowances fall to a basic amount.

****

10

Reaching Retirement Age

On reaching retirement age, it will be necessary to ensure that all paperwork relating to pension contributions is in order. There are a number of rules that should be observed in order to ensure that any pension due is paid:

- keep all documents relating to pension rights
- start organising any pension due before retirement, this will ensure that any problems are overcome well before retirement

It is very important that communication is kept with all pension providers, and that they have accurate up-to-date records of a person's whereabouts. Each time addresses are changed this should be communicated to all pension providers. If it is impossible to track down an old employer from whom a pension is due, the Pension Schemes Registry can help. This was set up in 1990, by the government to help people trace so-called 'lost pensions'. If help is needed this can be obtained by filling in form PR4 which can be obtained from the Pensions Advisory Service or the Pensions Scheme Registry.

How to claim state pension

A letter will be sent to all retiree's about four months before retirement date. This will come from the pension service and will detail how much pension is due. The pension is not paid automatically, it has to be claimed. This can be done by phoning the Pensions Claim Line number included with the letter, or by filling in a claim form BR1. If the person is a married man and the wife is claiming based on the husbands contributions, then form BF225 should be filled in.

If the pension is to be deferred it is advisable to contact the Pensions Service in writing as soon as possible.

A late pension claim can be backdated up to twelve months. If a man is claiming for a pension for his wife based on his contributions this can only be backdated six-months.

How the pension is paid

Pensions are paid by the DWP pension direct to a bank account or Post Office Card Account. To find out more about the payment of pensions contact the DWP Direct Payment Information Line.

Leaving the country

If a person goes abroad for less than six months, they can carry on receiving pension in the normal way. If the trip is for longer then the Pension Service should be contacted and one of the following arrangements can be made to pay a pension:

- have it paid into a personal bank account while away
- arrange for it to be paid into a Post Office Card Account
- arrange for the money to be paid abroad

If a person is living outside of the UK at the time of the annual pension increase they won't qualify for the increase unless they reside in a member country of the European Union or a country with which the UK has an agreement for increasing pensions. It is very important that you check what will happen to your state pension when you move abroad. The DWP International Pension Centre can help.

Pensions from an occupational scheme

Although different schemes have different arrangements, there are similar rules for each scheme. About three months before a person reaches normal retirement age, they should contact the scheme. Either telephone or write enclosing all the details that they will need. The following questions should be asked:

- what pension is due?
- what is the lump-sum entitlement?
- how will the pension be reduced if a lump sum is taken?
- How will the pension be paid, will there be any choices as to frequency?

- Is there a widow's or widowers pension, and if so how will it affect the retirement pension?
- Are there any pensions for other dependants in the event of death?

If a person has been making Additional Voluntary Contributions, then a detailed breakdown of these will be needed.

Retiring early

Retirement earlier than the normal age for a scheme may result in payment of a pension at an earlier age. The minimum age for a pension is 50 with the exception of retirement on ill-health grounds. A scheme administrator will be able to supply full details.

Retiring late

Depending on the rules of the occupational scheme it may be possible to delay retirement and take the pension later. Again, the scheme administrators can help.

Method of payment

Depending on how the pension is arranged, it may be paid direct from the provider or via an insurance company. The usual for pension payments is either quarterly or monthly in advance into a personal bank account. The scheme administrators will be able to provide more information with regard to this.

A pension from a personal plan

In the same way as a pension from an occupational scheme, it is necessary to get in touch with the pension provider about 3-4 months before retirement date. The main questions that should be asked are:

- how much is the pension fund worth?
- how much pension will the plan provider offer?
- can an increase be arranged each year and if so how much is the increase?
- what is the maximum lump sum?
- is there a widow's or widowers or other dependants pension?
- what are the other options if any?
- can the purchase of an annuity be deferred without affecting the drawing of an income?

Pensions can only be paid by an insurance company or a friendly society so if the pension has been with any other form of provider then it has to be switched before it can be paid.

If there are protected-rights from a contracted out pension plan, these can be, may have to be, treated quite separately from the rest of a pension. Protected rights from a personal pension cannot be paid until a person has reached 60 years of age. A person must, by law, have an open market option enabling protected rights pension to be paid by another provider, if it is desired.

Choosing the right annuity

It is very important that an open market option is exercised at retirement. Advice should be obtained from a specialist annuity advisor. If husband and wife, it may be advisable to take out a joint annuity which will carry on paying out an income until the last partner dies, otherwise a widower or widow could be left in financial hardship.

One popular option is an annuity that pays a guaranteed income for five-years. The usual annuity pays a lifetime income then stops on death. Another option is to take out an increasing annuity. This is compulsory for contracted-out pension rights, but otherwise optional.

As annuities have fallen over the years, another option is to take out a with-profits annuity. This is a higher risk option but offers a higher return. Income from a with-profits annuity is usually made up of two parts: a guaranteed basic payment and bonuses. At the time of taking out the annuity a person must choose the starting income which the annuity will provide. The choice will depend on the likely level of future bonuses (assumed bonuses ABR) and the degree of risk that can be borne. There is a choice between:

- low ABR (minimum 0% or no bonuses). The annuity income will start at a very low level. But as long as any bonus is declared the income will increase.
- higher ABR (maximum say 4%). The starting income will be higher. The higher the ABR that is chosen the greater the starting income. Each year, provided the

bonus that is declared is greater than the ABR that you chose, the income will increase. If the declared bonus is lower than the ABR, the income will fall back.

Annuity deferral and income withdrawal

Pension plans set up on or after 1st May 1995 can offer the option of annuity deferral and income withdrawal which allows a person to start taking an income from a pension plan but without buying an annuity. Instead, the income is drawn down direct from the pension fund. The remaining fund must be used to buy an annuity before the age of 75. The income must be reviewed every three years to ensure that the pension fund isn't being depleted too fast.

Payments of personal pensions

If the amount involved is very small then this can be taken as a lump sum. The amount is £2,500 or less or is too small to buy a £250 annuity income. Otherwise, the usual arrangements will apply, with you choosing the most convenient method of payment, by cheque, or payment monthly or quarterly into a bank account.

What happens to a company pension when you die?

What happens to your pension when you die depends on what type of scheme you have, its rules and whether you have already retired.

If you die before retirement-final salary schemes

What happens to your pension fund will depend on whether you are:

- an active member, i.e. you are still making contributions: or
- a deferred member-you have stopped making contributions (for example you have left the company) but haven't transferred your fund to another scheme.

Active members

Depending on your scheme's rules, a number of benefits may be payable, including:

- a return of all your contributions, usually repaid without interest:
- a tax free lump sum of up to four times your salary you were getting at the time of your death
- a pension for your spouse, civil partner or another dependant-often half, but as much as two thirds of the amount you would have got at pension age (as stated in the schemes rules).

These are maximum benefits, and many schemes pay lower amounts, so it's advisable to find out from your scheme administrator exactly what your scheme provides. Most schemes provide benefits for your spouse or civil partner, but if you have a partner and aren't legally married or in a civil partnership your scheme may not recognise them.

Deferred members

If you are a deferred member, your dependants often have fewer rights to benefits than if you were an active member, but again this depends on your scheme rules. You need to check with your scheme administrator.

Money purchase schemes

With money purchase schemes, the rules are generally the same whether you are an active or deferred member. Your pension fund will be refunded to your chosen beneficiary or you estate. If the scheme is contracted out of the second state pension, some of the benefit will usually be used to provide an income for your spouse or civil partner. There will often be a lump sum benefit provided by insurance cover too, but schemes vary widely and its advisable to check with your scheme administrator to find out exactly what your scheme provides.

'Expression of wish' forms

When you join a company's scheme, you will probably be asked to fill in an expression of wish form. This states who you would like any lump sum benefits to be paid to. The trustees of your scheme will usually make any final decision about who receives these benefits, but will usually follow what is said on the form. It is important to amend the form if your circumstances change.

If you die after you have retired

Most pensions have a guarantee period of five years. If you die within that time, the balance of the guarantee is paid, sometimes as a lump sum to the person who you have nominated or to your estate.

There may also be a pension payable to your husband or wife or civil partner usually for the rest of their life. It is important to check rules of the scheme as to who is entitled to receive that pension.

****

11

Pension Reforms

In 2007 and 2008 two new pensions Acts were introduced. These Acts were the result of a wide-ranging study of the current pensions system. Some of the changes have been referred to throughout this book. However, many of the changes wont come into effect until 2012 so are worth summarising here.

The 2007 Pensions Act

The Basic State pension

The key changes to the basic state pension include:

- reducing the number of qualifying years needed for a full basic state pension to 30 for people who will reach State pension age on or after 6th April 2010;
- any number of qualifying years will give entitlement to at least some basic State pension;
- people who have fewer than 30 qualifying years will get 1/30th of full basic state pension for each qualifying year they have;
- both paid and credited National Insurance Contributions will count towards basic state pension in the same way;

- replacing the system of Home responsibilities Protection (HRP) with a new weekly National Insurance Credit for people caring for children or severely disabled people and converting past years of Home responsibilities Protection into years of credits;
- increasing basic state pension in line with earnings rather than prices which means that it should rise more quickly each year than it does now.

State Second Pension

The State Second Pension is paid in addition to the basic state pension. Key changes to this pension will include:

- allowing people to combine national Insurance contributions from earnings in part of a tax year with credits for other parts of the same year in order to gain a qualifying year for State Second Pension;
- making it easier for people caring for children or severely disabled people to build up entitlement;
- changing the way it builds up so that in the future it will provide a simple flat rate weekly top up to the basic state pension

Working and caring will be recognised equally in the reformed State Pension scheme, with more women and carers being eligible for a full basic State Pension and second State Pension. From 6th April 2010, more people who are not paying National Insurance Contributions will be able to build up basic entitlement to State Pension and Second State Pension through a new weekly NI credit.

The people who will be eligible for these new credits are:

- people who are getting Child benefit for children up to the age of 12
- approved foster carers
- caring for at least 20 hours a week for people who are getting attendance allowance, Disability Living Allowance or Constant Attendance Allowance
- having caring responsibility for at least 20 hours a week for other people who need care.

People who pay NI contributions for part of a tax year and qualify for the new credits for the rest of the tax year will be able to combine them to gain a qualifying year for basic State Pension and State Second Pension.

State Pension age

At present the age at which men and women can claim state pension is different. Men get their state pension from 65 but, until April 2010, women can get theirs at 60. State pension age for women will increase to 65, phased in from 2010 so that by 2020 the age will be the same for men and women.

The age that both men and women can receive pension will rise in stages between 2024 and 2046 from 65 to 68.

Other state pension changes

People who claim state pension on or after 6th April 2010 will not be able to claim extra money for their spouse or civil partner. People who are already getting this money (known as adult dependency increase) before April 2010 will keep it, but only until 2020 at the latest.

From 6th April 2010, a married or separated woman who needs to use her husbands National Insurance contributions for her pension will be able to claim this once both she and her husband have reached state pension age. She won't have to wait until he has actually claimed his pension. The same applies to a married man whose wife or civil partner was born after 5th April 1950, if they need to use their wife's or civil partners contributions.

For more details of the changes which will be enacted under this acts you should go to the Department of Works and pensions website.

The Pensions Act 2008

The Pensions Act 2008 contains a number of measures aimed at encouraging greater private pension saving. From 2012 it is planned that all eligible workers who are not already in a good quality workplace scheme will be automatically enrolled into their employers pension scheme or a new savings vehicle, which is currently known as a personal account scheme. To encourage participation, employees pension contributions will be supplemented by contributions from employers and tax relief.

Automatic enrolment

It is planned that from 2012, employers will automatically enrol eligible workers who are not in a qualifying scheme into an automatic enrolment scheme (which can include the new personal accounts scheme). Automatic enrolment means instead of choosing whether to join a workplace pension scheme provided by their employer, all eligible worker will have to actively decide to not be in a scheme, if for any reason they feel this is not a suitable form of saving for their situation.

Minimum employer contribution

For the first time all employers will be required to contribute a minimum of 3% (on a band of earnings) to an eligible employee's workplace pension scheme. This will supplement the 3% contribution from the employee and around 1% from the Government in the form of tax relief.

The Act also includes other measures. To obtain more details of the Act you should go to www.thepensionservice.gov.uk

****

12

Continuing to Work

So far, this book has been about taking care to provide for your pension, and also when and how to draw it when the time is right. The time may not be right at the official retirement age. This is very much an individual decision and you have the right to carry on working.

On the 1st of October 2006, new legislation came into effect in the UK to effectively ban age discrimination in the workplace. Many workplaces, particularly those within the public sector have had policies in place for years to ensure that age discrimination is outlawed. However, now, beyond the age of 65 you have the right to ask to stay on and your employer to consider your request. The upshot is that your employer can turn you down and does not have to give a reason why. This makes a bit of a nonsense of the legislation although you now have the right to ask, whereas before this did not exist.

Changing your job

There is nothing to stop you drawing a pension from one employer's scheme and then taking up employment elsewhere. The age discrimination rules apply to recruitment and so place a general ban on turning down an applicant on the basis of age. However, there are various exceptions. You can be turned down legally because of age if you are older than 65 (or the employers normal retirement age if younger) or you are within six months of reaching that age. If there are objective grounds for turning you down then the employer can do so. One such ground is that you may not be able to work for a reasonably long enough period after training. Finally, if there is a genuine occupational reason for turning you down such as needing a younger person to act in a role.

Running your own business

Retirement can be an opportunity to start your own business, perhaps turning a hobby into a business or trying something else completely new. This could be pursuing a dream, such as buying and selling property, self-publishing or whatever you have been developing or thinking about but didn't have the time to do when you were working.

Choosing the right business for you is not just a matter of thinking about the skills that you have. You should give serious thought to the work/life balance that you want to create. Some business take up a lot of time and can create a lot of stress, such as purchasing a shop. This in particular is likely to dominate your time and should, realistically, be avoided, unless you are absolutely certain about what you want to sell and where.

Business structure and tax

One of the first decisions is whether to set up a company, work in a partnership or go self-employed. By far the easiest route is to be self-employed. There are no formalities, such as setting up a company. You simply start trading, although you must register your business with HM Revenue and Customs within three months of the end of the month in which you start trading. You will have to fill in a tax return after the end of each tax year. Any profit that you make is added to your other income-such as pensions and any taxable investment income-to see if the total is high enough for you to have to pay tax.

Partnerships

From a tax point of view, partnerships are treated the same way as being self-employed. As with being self-employed, you have three months to register that you have started up and must complete an annual tax return. You should always try to have a formal agreement with any partners and get a solicitor to draw it up.

Trading as a company

This is the most top-heavy way of trading and there are a number of formalities to go through. These include forming a company, choosing a name and registering the company with Companies House who will require you to send in an annual return and also accounts each year. You will also need to contact your local tax office to tell them that you have started trading. By far and away the simplest form of business structure is that of self-employed and you should go this route if possible.

****

13

Extras because of age

When you reach the age of 60, you are automatically entitled to various concessions, such as travel, prescriptions and help with health care.

Travel

If you are aged 60 or over and live in England, Scotland and Wales you are automatically entitled to travel free on local buses. If you live in Northern Ireland, trains are covered as well. The schemes will vary across the country and different local authorities have the right to offer additional concessions. The table below gives you an idea of the current concessions on offer.

SCHEME	AGE ELIGIBILITY	WHERE YOU CAN TRAVEL	TRAVEL TIME RESTRICTION	MORE INFO
England: National Bus Pass	60 and over	Local buses throughout England	Not peak hours (before 9.30 weekdays)	Local authority
Wales: Concessionary Bus Pass	60 and over	Local buses throughout Wales	None	Local authority
Scotland: National Entitlement Card	60 and over	Local buses and scheduled coaches throughout Scotland	None	Local authority, Post office or Strathclyde Partnership for Transport Centre
Northern Ireland 60+ smart pass	60-64	Buses and Trains throughout Northern Ireland	None	Translink Tel 028 90 66 66 30 or bus and rail stations

Northern Ireland Senior Smart Pass	65 and over	Buses and trains throughout Northern Ireland and Cross Border Travel	None	Translink or bus and rail stations

Coaches

Some coach companies offer discounted fares on national routes to travellers over 60 (National express, Scottish Citylink, Berry's and Baker Dolphin). People aged over 60 and over can buy a Senior Railcard which entitles them to one-third off most fares for rail travel throughout Britain.

Passport

If you were born on or before 2nd September 1929, you no longer have to pay for your passport. You can ask for a refund if you are eligible and have applied for a replacement passport since 19th May 2004.

Health

NHS Prescriptions. Once you reach age 60 you qualify for free NHS prescriptions (Currently £7.10 in 2009/10). If you are eligible you simply sign the declaration on the back of the prescription. Scotland and Northern Ireland have stated that they will be phasing out charges for prescriptions, which will become free for everyone from April 2010 (Northern Ireland) and April 2010 (Scotland). Prescriptions are already free for all in Wales.

NHS sight tests. From age 60 you also qualify for free NHS sight tests but you still have to pay for the glasses and lenses, unless your income is low. You can get free sight tests from age 40 if you are considered at risk of developing glaucoma because a close family member has this condition (or any age if you already have sight problems).

Help with bills

Winter fuel payments. This scheme is in force all over the UK and provides a cash sum to every household with one or more people over 60 in the 'qualifying week' which is the week beginning the third Monday in September. You can use the cash in any way you like. However, it is designed specifically to help you cope with Winter fuel bills. The standard payment is normally £200 per household or £300 for households with someone 80 or over.

Television licence. Anyone aged 75 or over can apply for a free television licence. It doesn't matter if there are younger people in the household but the licence must be in the name of the person aged 75 or over. If you are already a licence holder you can apply for a cheaper licence for the part year that you turn 75. The licence lasts three years at a time and you should re-apply after three years.

Your home

You can get help with heating and fuel efficiency if you are aged 60 or over.

Heating rebate over £300. This is operated under the name Warm Front in England (see useful addresses for equivalent schemes in UK). The eligibility conditions are that you are aged 60 or over, own your own home or rent privately and you have no central heating or the system you have does not work. You get a voucher/claim form to use when an approved supplier fits a new heating system. You can also get free insulation if you are 70 or over. You are entitled to free loft and cavity wall insulation under a Central Government scheme. You should check out your local authority and local energy suppliers who may also offer schemes.

Repairs and Improvements

One of the most important elements of your home is that of its condition. When you retire or are close to retiring, this presents the ideal opportunity to assess the overall condition of your home and to draw up a condition survey (or have one drawn up) so that you can plan expenditure. It is wise to commence the work as soon as possible after retirement, or before if possible, so that you can still carry out works yourself, without resorting to using building firms. This will save money and mean that you have more control. This chapter also points the way to the various agencies that exist who will give you advice on repairs and maintenance and also funding.

Deciding what needs to be carried out

There are specialist advice agencies, called Home Improvement Agencies (sometimes called Care and Repair or Staying Put) that will give specialist advice to older and vulnerable householders and also to people living in private rented accommodation. They are small scale, no-for-profit organisations, usually managed locally by housing associations, councils or charities. They will usually offer practical help with tasks such as arranging a condition survey, getting estimates from builders (trusted builders) applying for grants or loans and also keeping an eye on the progress of work. They may charge a fee towards their assistance, which is usually included in the grant or loans that you may be in receipt of.

To find out whether there is a home improvement agency in your area, you should contact your local Age Concern or the local council housing department or Foundations (the National Co-ordinating Body for Home Improvement Agencies). Address at the rear of the book.

If there is no Home Improvement Agency in your area you might want to engage a surveyor to carry one out for you. As these are costly, or can be, you should always ask what the cost will be first. The Chartered Surveyor Voluntary Service exists to help people who would other wise be able to get professional advice. You need to be referred to them by a Citizens Advice Bureau first.

Finding a Builder

If there is no Home Improvement Agency in your area, you should take care, great care, when trying to find a good reliable builder. We have all heard stories of rogue builders who carry out shoddy work and charge over the odds. If you intend to employ a builder, particularly for a larger job, then you should always employ a builder backed by a proper guarantee scheme. The Federation of Master Builders (FMB) offers a MasterBond

Planning For the Future-Managing Retirement Finances

Warranty: its members must meet certain criteria and adhere to the FMB's Code of Practice. The ten-year insurance backed warranty will add 1.5% to the total cost of a job but is money well spent.

Information on this scheme can be obtained from the FMB website at www.fmb.org.uk.

To ensure that you get a good job done, the FMB recommends that you:

- Always ask for references and names of previous clients
- Get estimates from two or three builders
- Ask for the work to be covered by an insurance backed warranty
- Get a written specification and quotation
- Use a contract (the FMB has a plain English contract for small works)
- Agree any staged and final payments before a job
- Avoid dealing in cash

The FMB has played a leading role in the development of the government backed TrustMark scheme, which is a consumer protection initiative for the home repair and improvement sector.

A wide range of traders, including plumbers and electricians, are being licensed to become TrustMark registered firms. For more information contact TrustMark. Address at the rear of this book.

78

Financial help with repairs and improvements

Sometimes, individuals find themselves in a position where they cannot afford repairs to their homes. There are, however, various forms of assistance at hand. Local authorities have general powers to provide help with repairs and also adaptations to housing. The assistance isn't always cash based, it can also be provided in the form of labour material or advice. The cash element will usually be either grants or loans. Local authorities will have published policies explaining the various forms of assistance. These can vary from time to time, as many of them are dependant on national legislation and government funding. Below are a few of the types of grants available.

Disabled facilities grant

These grants provide facilities and adaptations to help a disabled person to live as independently and in as much comfort as possible. They are means tested (i.e.) dependant on income, with the exception of grants for disabled children. In its assessment, the council will take into account only your income and that of your partner or spouse. If you receive the guarantee part of Pension Credit, income Support or income based Jobseeker's allowance you will not normally have to make any contribution. People receiving Working or Child Tax Credit (with gross taxable income of less than £15,000) have these payments disregarded as income. The grant is usually mandatory provided that your home needs adaptations to enable you to use essential facilities such as kitchen or bathroom. The maximum amount of grant is £30,000. You can get more information about these grants from your local authority housing department.

If you receive Pension credit, Income Support or Income based jobseekers allowance, you may be able to get a Community Care Grant or Budgeting Loan from the Social fund to help you with the cost of minor repairs.

Social services departments provide funding for some minor adaptation works. They may also be able to help with some types of work not covered by the disabled facilities grant.

If you want to raise capital from your home to pay for works, the Home Improvement Trust may be able to help. It is a not-for-profit company that has links with a number of commercial lenders who provide older people with low cost loans raised against the value of their home. You can contact Home Improvement Trust direct at the address at the rear of the book.

The Care and Repair England publication also provides useful information about organising and financing building works. You can get a copy by phoning 0115 950 6500 or by downloading it from the website www.careandrepair-england.org.uk.

Adapting your home

You may need to make certain adaptations to your home if you or a member of your family needs them, such as mobility aids, to make it easier to navigate the house. There are other areas that can be helpful, such as the positioning of the furniture. Occupational Therapists can give detailed advice. They can assess a persons mobility and their ability to move around and can provide appropriate advice. You should contact your local social services department and ask for an assessment of needs. You don't have to have a letter from the doctor but this can speed things up. Social services should provide some equipment free if you or a relative is assessed as needing them. All minor adaptations costing less than £1000 must be provided free of charge.

For full information about special equipment and furniture, contact the Disabled Living Foundation at the address at the rear of the book.

****

14

Raising Capital from your Home

Equity release schemes

The main principle behind equity release schemes, which enable you to release cash from your home, is that you are offered a lump sum or an income now but you, or your estate, have to pay back a larger sum to compensate the investors (the Equity release companies). This amounts to a longer term loan which is paid back later with rolled up interest. If you wish to raise money but do not wish to move home then these schemes could be for you.

Equity release schemes come in two basic forms: lifetime mortgages and home reversion schemes.

Lifetime mortgages

With a lifetime mortgage you borrow against the value of your home but the capital, and usually the interest are repaid only on your death or when you move out. Lifetime mortgages can be taken out jointly with your spouse or partner, in which case the loan does not have to be repaid until the second death. You can use a lifetime mortgage to raise a single large cash sum. If you want an income you can draw out a series of smaller sums or use a single lump sum to buy an investment, such as an annuity. The former is more tax efficient because the income from an annuity is usually taxable.

Types of lifetime mortgages

With the most common form of lifetime loan-a roll up loan-interest is added each month to the amount that you owe. You are charged interest not just on the amount that you originally borrowed, but to the increasing balance as interest is added. The interest can be fixed for the whole life of the loan or can be variable. When your home is eventually sold, the proceeds are used to repay the outstanding loan and what is left over goes to your estate. Different providers set different age limits but you must be at least 55 or 60 with most schemes to be eligible for a lifetime mortgage. In addition, the value of your home, less any debts secured against it must be in the region of £50,000 and upwards. If you have an existing mortgage you will usually be required to pay this off with the loan. The amounts that you can borrow will vary with your age. The maximum for a roll up loan is usually about half the value.

Reversion schemes

With a reversion scheme you sell part or all of your home, but retain the right to live there either rent free or for a token rent. When the home is eventually sold, the reversionary company takes a percentage of the sale proceeds, or the whole amount if you sold 100 per cent of your home. This means that the reversion company, as opposed to the estate gets the benefit of any increase in value of your home. A reversion scheme can be taken out singly or jointly, in which case it continues until the second death.

As with lifetime mortgages reversion schemes can pay you a single lump sum or a series of smaller lump sums. Alternatively, they may be combined with an annuity or other investment to provide you with a regular income. Investment income is usually taxable but lump sums from the sale of your home are not. The money that you get when you take out the loan will be smaller than the value of the part of your home that you sell. This difference represents the return to the reversionary company. A key factor that the reversionary company uses in deciding what it will offer is how long it expects to have to wait before it gets its money back. To qualify for a reversionary scheme you will usually be between 65-70. Your home must be in reasonable condition and worth a minimum amount, typically £75,000.

Alternatives to equity release

One of the most common reasons for considering equity release is to raise extra income for day to day living. If this is your main motive, you might want to consider ensuring that the other avenues for raising income have been explored. For example:

- Are you claiming all the state benefits due to you, such as Pension Credit, Council Tax Benefit and Attendance Allowance
- Have you taken steps to trace any lost pensions that you might be claiming?

- Are you exploiting the potential of your home, for example taking in a lodger?
- Are you making sure that you are not overspending?
- Are you paying too much tax?

You cannot normally use equity release to raise a lump sum of below £10,000. If such a sum is needed you might want to consider taking out an interest only mortgage. Unlike a lifetime mortgage you pay interest each month so the amount borrowed does not grow.

The main thing with equity release schemes is that you should get good advice, usually independent advice so that you are totally aware of what it is that you are signing up for.

****

15

Selling your home

As we all know, the housing market has undergone one of its periodic 'corrections' and the value of property has once again plummeted. This time it has been in the context of one of the worst recessions in living memory. Therefore, the wisdom of using your home, or factoring in your home, as a source of income when retirement age is reached, is questionable.

Falling property prices are just one of the problems if your intention is to sell up to release capital for your retirement. The other main one is that if you are aiming to downsize to a smaller home then the price of this property may not necessarily be that much cheaper than the family home that you are selling. This does depend of course on the nature, size and value of that property. In addition, there are also the other problems associated with relocating, such as getting used to a new area, neighbours and so on.

You should bear in mind as well that there are significant costs associated with selling, moving and buying. This will eat into any equity that you release from your property and should be taken into account.

The table overleaf will give you an idea of the costs involved.

	COST	EXAMPLE 1. SELLING A HOME FOR £250,000 AND BUYING FOR £150,000	EXAMPLE 2. SELLING A HOME FOR £600,000 AND BUYING FOR £250,000
AS A SELLER			
ESTATE AGENTS FEE	1.5%-2% OF SELLING PRICE	£4375	£10,500
HOME INFORMATION PACK	£350	£350	£350
AS A BUYER			
STAMP DUTY LAND TAX	SEE TABLE BELOW	£0	£2500
SURVEYORS FEE	APPROX £500	£500	£500
SEARCH FEES AND LAND REGISTRY FEES	APPROX £500	£500	£500
AS BOTH			
LEGAL COSTS	APPROX £1500	£1500	£1500
REMOVAL COSTS	£600	£600	£600
TOTAL		**£7825**	**£16,450**

Case study

John and Doreen

John and Doreen are selling a £350,000 family home and buying a flat for £200,000. The costs for downsizing are:

- Estate agents fees 1.5% £5250
- Home Information pack £350
- Stamp duty land tax 1% £2000
- Survey £500
- Search fees, Land Registry etc £500
- Legal costs on both sales and purchase £1500
- Removal costs £600

Total £10,700 The cash realised from downsizing is £350,000-£200,000-£10,700 = £139,300.

The main advantage of downsizing is that you realise the full value of the home that you are selling (apart from costs). Also, if you are selling your own home the proceeds are tax-free.

****

16

Income Tax

Tax basics

Each person in the UK is taxed as an individual. Tax is based on income for a tax year. Whilst some types of income is tax free, other income is potentially taxable. Income that is taxable includes earnings from a job you may have, any profits from self employment or business, state and private pensions, some benefits and any other income such as rents receivable, savings interest, dividends from shares etc.

Tax relief can be obtained on certain types of spending which is given in two ways:

- By deducting the expense from your total income, thus reducing the amount of income left to be taxed. This applies to contributions to occupational pension schemes and donations to charity through payroll giving
- Through tax relief at source. You deduct tax relief from the payment you are making and handover the remaining reduced amount. If you are a higher rate taxpayer, you can claim extra relief. This method applies to contributions to personal pensions and chartable donations to gift aid.

Personal allowances

Every individual has a personal allowance. There are annually published individual allowances, which may vary according to individual circumstances.

The table below shows the annual allowances applicable for 2009/10. The allowances are higher for people aged between 65-74 and higher again for people over 75. However, you will lose this extra age-related allowance if your income exceeds the threshold shown below. The extra allowance is reduced by £1 for every £2 by which your income exceeds the threshold until it is reduced to the level of the under 65 allowance.

Income tax personal allowances

		2009/10
Under 65		£6,475
65-74		£9,490
75 or over		£9,640
Income threshold at which age related allowance starts to be lost		£22,900
Income level at which all the age related allowance is lost and you just get the under 65 allowance*		

65-74		£28,930
75 or over		£29,230
* This income level will be higher if you are married or in a civil partnership and you or your spouse or partner were born before 6 April 1935 (see married couples allowance overleaf)		

Income tax rates and bands

Allowances for blind people

A blind person's allowance is available if you are registered blind in England or would be unable to carry out any work for which normal eyesight is needed (Scotland and Northern Ireland). In either case, this means that you have been certified as blind or severely sight impaired by a consultant opthalmologist. The allowance is £1890 in 2009/10.

If your income is too low for you to be able to use all or part of your blind person's allowance, you can request your tax office to transfer the surplus to your spouse or civil partner to reduce their tax burden.

The Married Couple's allowance

This particular allowance is restricted to married couples and civil partners where one or both of the couple were born before 6th April 1935. In 2009/10 the allowance is £6965. Married couples allowance works differently to other allowances in that you get a reduction in your tax bill equal to 10% of the allowance or the amount needed to reduce your tax bill to zero (whichever is lower). Married couples allowance is initially given to the husband (if you were married before 5th December 2005 or whoever has the higher income where your marriage or civil partnership took place on or after that date). If the person who has the allowance has income above the age related allowance threshold (£22,900 in 2009/10) the married couple's allowance is reduced by £1 for every £2 of income over the threshold. However, married couples allowance is never reduced below a basic amount (£2670 in 2009/10). Age related personal allowance is reduced before any married couples allowance. Whoever initially gets the married couples allowance, part or all of the basic amount can be transferred to the other spouse or partner.

Tax-free income
These are the main types of income likely to be relevant in later life that are free from income tax.

Pensions and state benefits

- £10 Christmas bonus for state pensioners and also the one-off £60 Christmas bonus introduced in 2009-09-14
- Winter fuel payment
- Pension credit
- Working tax credit
- Housing benefit
- Bereavement payment (lump sum for widows and widowers)
- Council tax benefit
- Disability living allowance and attendance allowance
- Any additional occupational pensions arising as a result of injury at work
- Tax free lump sum from a pension scheme

Income from an employer

- Some fringe benefits, such as employers pensions contributions
- Mileage allowance
- Up to £30,000 redundancy payment
- Up to £3 a week to cover the extra cost of working from home
- Long service award that is not cash and has been given for £20 or more years service
- Lump sum death benefit from life insurance provided through work

Savings and investments

- Interest from National Savings and Investments including premium bonds
- Interest from ISA's
- Interest from savings and bond based investments held in stocks and shares ISA's, CTF's and tax efficient friendly society plans
- That part of the income from a purchased life annuity that represents the return of your capital
- Income from an annuity paid direct to a care provider
-

Other income

- Up to £4250 from letting room(s) in your home through the rent a room scheme
- Payouts from mortgage payment protection policies and other loan protection policies
- Payout from an income protection policy you have arranged for yourself (but not such insurance provided by your employer)
- Payout to your survivors from a term insurance policy following your death.

****

17

Capital Gains Tax

Some types of assets do not attract a capital gain. These are listed below. With those assets that do attract capital gains Tax, the first step in working out what tax there is to pay, if any, is to take the final value, the proceeds of sale, and deduct the amount you paid, known as the initial value. However, if you give the asset away, or it was given to you, instead you will need to use the market value on the date of the gift. Also, if you began owning the asset before 31st March 1982, you can substitute the market value on that date for the actual initial value. You are allowed to deduct a number of expenses, including the following:

- Costs of buying and selling
- Costs of defending your title to the asset
- Amounts spent on the item to improve its state and enhance its value.

If the final value less initial value and allowable losses comes to less than zero you have made a loss. This must be set against any gains you make on the disposal of other assets during the same tax year. But losses that cannot be set off in this way are then carried forward for use in future tax years.

Reliefs

There is no capital gains Tax on a gain or part of a gain that is covered by tax relief. The situations outlined below are common situations faced by people who are retiring:

Retiring from business

If you are self employed or run a company you will need to decide what to do with your business when you retire. There are a number of things that you can do, give the business away sell the business, shut it down.

Giving the business away

If you give the business away to an individual or a trust you and the new owner can jointly claim hold-over relief from CGT. This means that any gain that you have made while owning the business is transferred to the new owner by deducting it from the initial value at which they are treated as having acquired the business. When the new owner disposes of the business, the gain is worked out using this adjusted value. Hold over relief is not given automatically and you and the new owner must make a joint claim within five years of the 31st January following the end of the tax year in which the business was transferred.

Selling your business or closing it down

If you sell your business as a going concern or shut it down and sell off the assets within the next three years you may be able to claim entrepeneurs relief. This allows you to ignore 4/9ths of any gain-in effect reducing the tax payable from 18%

to 10%. However, the business gains over your whole lifetime (since 6th April 2008) on which you can claim this relief are limited to £1million. Relief is not given automatically. You must claim it within one year of 31st January following the tax year in which the business was sold or disposed of.

Selling your home

In general there is no CGT on selling your main residence. In some situations however, private residence relief might be restricted, for example if you are absent from your home for long periods or use part of your home exclusively for business or have let your home. Some periods away from home do not cause a reduction in private residence relief:

- The first year of ownership in which you might be renovating your home or rebuilding the property
- The last three years of ownership
- Periods of any length when you were working abroad
- Periods when you live in job related accommodation elsewhere
- Any other periods of absence that together add up to no more than three years as long as you lived in the home both before the first absence and after the last.

Losses

Any losses that you make on selling or giving away assets must be deducted from gains made in the same tax year. Once the gains made are reduced to zero, any remaining losses are carried forward to future years. Having deducted all your expenses, reliefs and losses you can, you next subtract your annual tax free allowance and pay CGT at a single rate of 18% on whatever remains.

Capital Gains Tax free gains

The below are the most common gains and transactions on which you do not have to pay CGT:

- Whatever you leave on death, although Inheritance tax may be payable
- Gifts to your spouse or civil partner, provided that you live together
- Gifts to charity and local sports clubs that are eligible to be treated in the same way as charities
- Your only or main home
- Private cars
- Assets that are deemed to have a life of 50 years or less (wasting assets)
- More durable personal belongings with a personal value of less than £6000.
- Foreign currency for personal spending and British money
- Gambling and lottery wins
- Gains on certain investments, including ISA's or Child Trust Funds, Gilts and many corporate bonds.

18

Future Care options

As is well documented over a third of people over 65-74 and over a half over the age of 75 have a long standing health condition that affects their lives in some way. The ability to carry on living in ones own home really depends a lot on the availability of appropriate care. Quite often this is not readily available, and comes at a cost. Those who are fortunate enough can be cared for by their family.

In 1993, the government introduced policies designed to help more people live independently in their own homes through the expansion of formal support services. This has had the effect of reducing the number of people who need care home support.

However, we are living in an age of an increasing elderly population and there is increase pressure on finances and the ability of government to pay. Whether you are thinking of support in the future for an aging relative or indeed for yourself, there are several main factors that you need to consider and decisions to be made:

- Exactly what form of care might be needed in the future, whether a retirement home or higher level sheltered housing

- Where will the money come from to pay for the care?

We need now to examine the various options available.

Care in the home

Most people would rather stay in their own home and receive the appropriate level of support for their needs. Regardless of your own personal financial situation you have the right to approach social services in your local authority area for a needs assessment. Then a manager from the department will visit you in your home (or relative as case may be) and put together a care plan for you. There are usually a number of components to such a plan, for example:

- Visits in your home on a daily basis, if needed, and to address specific requirements such as climbing stairs or getting into bed
- Help with housework and shopping
- Organising equipment such as stair rails, ramps etc to assist mobility
- Provision of an emergency call service, usually run by a local authority or housing association
- Day centre activities so you can socialise
- Mobile meals service-meals on wheels have largely been replaced by delivery of frozen foods.

Whilst some smaller items of equipment can be provide free many of the items in the care plan have to be paid for. This will be means tested.

There are certain fundamental rules that local authorities must abide by. Charges should not reduce the income that a person has left below a set level. If a person is 60 or over, this is the Pension Credit Guarantee credit level plus a buffer which is dependant where you live in the UK, for example 25% in England and 35% in Wales.

Income for the purposes of assessment can include any disability related benefits such as attendance allowance, but the local authority should also take into account any disability related expenditure you may have over and above paying for the local authorities care services. Savings are taken into account when assessing ability to pay. Capital below a certain level (2008/9 £13,500 England and Northern Ireland, £19,000 Wales or £13,000 Scotland). If your capital is over a set level you will be charged the full amount for services (£22,250 England and Northern Ireland, £22,000 Wales, £21,500 Scotland) Between the lower and upper capital limits, you are assumed to receive £1 a week income for each £250 or part £250 of capital. Your home is not included as part of this capital.

The assessment should be based only on your income and generally not that of your partner or anyone else. If you feel that you are paying too much for your care services then you have the right to ask the local authority to review your financial assessment.

How the care is paid for
Either the local authority will pay you direct in cash for your services or, if you so desire, you can ask the local authority to

arrange and pay for the care. The Government has also been piloting a new scheme called Individual Budgets which is similar to Direct Payment, so you receive a cash sum, but it covers a wide range of services so it includes, for example, help towards a warden in sheltered housing. The aim of cash payments is to put the individual in more control of the services that they buy. Obviously, this may not be suited to everyone and some people will be more reliant on the local authority to provide and pay for services.

Other benefits available

There are other benefits available such as Disability Living Allowance or if you are over 65 Attendance Allowance. These benefits are tax-free and are not means tested. If you are a carer, you will also have the right to a free needs assessment to pay for extra levels of need. The care plan devised by the local authority might for example recommend that someone be paid for sitting with a relative whilst you have a few hours off, or respite care (where the disabled person moves temporarily into a care home). You will be expected to pay for these services unless your income and savings are low .

Retirement housing

Retirement housing is known by a number of different names that usually reflects the level of care needed, for example sheltered housing, warden assisted housing or warden controlled housing. This is designed for people over 60 (sometimes can be 55). Usually, it is a scheme that comprises a number of flats and maybe a few bungalows with communal areas for residents, such as lounge and gardens and in some cases a kitchen for the provision of communal meals. There is also usually a laundry area and an emergency call system plus a warden if included in the overall scheme cost.

Some schemes are private, people buy a lease, known as leasehold schemes for the elderly. Sheltered housing to rent is normally provided by local authorities and, more usually now, housing associations. To qualify for these schemes you have to prove that you are in need and cannot afford to buy. You may qualify for Housing Benefit.

Charges for retirement homes

The main cost associated with retirement housing, whether rented or owned, is the service charge. As an ex care home manager myself, I have long experience of the difficulties that surround service charges.

The service charge covers the cost of wardens, communal areas, emergency call system and gardening. Many other areas are included. If you are on a low income then you might be eligible for housing benefit for some of the services.

Ordinary sheltered housing does not include care services, this has to be arranged with your local authority. However, as discussed, sheltered housing can be more intensive and the levels of charges will reflect this. For example do you, or a relative envisage needing intensive care of a kind provided by category one sheltered housing or will you need a lesser degree of care?

Moving to a care home

If you move to a care home to receive personal care you may have to pay some or all of the fees yourself, depending on your income. If your main aim is health care, the NHS should pay. This is called NHS continuing care. In some circumstances, you may receive care at home either to avoid admission to hospital or to enable you to leave hospital early. In this case, you are entitled to free care-called intermediate care-which may include a mix of health and social care. The social care element should be free for a maximum of six weeks.

If your primary reason for moving to a care home is for help with personal care such as getting up, going to bed, bathing and so on, in general you are expected to pay for the fees yourself unless your income and savings are low. In that case, the local authority will carry out a financial assessment to determine whether you should pay anything at all. This assessment is in line with the capital limits stated previously.

Even if your main need is personal care, you may require some nursing care as well and this is provided free up to set limits depending where you live in the UK and, in England, on the extent of the nursing care that you need. For 2008/9 the limits are:

- England: a standard rate of £103.80 a week and a higher rate of £142.80 depending on the extent of nursing care that you need
- Wales: £117.66 per week
- Scotland: £67 per week

- Northern Ireland £100 per week

The Government pays these sums direct to your care provider. If you are paying for your care home fees yourself, you are likely to qualify for Attendance Allowance. If the NHS or local authority is paying for some or all of the fees, you will not be able to get Attendance Allowance as well.

Assessing your finances

Whether or not you can get state funding depends in part on how much capital you have. Capital includes savings and investments but can also include your house. However, if your partner (married or not), an elderly or disabled relative or a child under 16 still lives there, the value of your home is disregarded. The local authority also has the discretion to ignore your home, if, for example, you carer will carry on living there.

If you are a couple, the local authority is not allowed to base the financial assessment on your joint resources. It must consider only the capital and income that belongs to you. If you are holding assets on behalf of someone else you must prove that they are not your assets or the local authority will treat them as your assets. You can be treated as still owning capital if you are deemed to have deliberately deprived yourself of it. This could be the case if you have given away assets to other family members in advance of applying for a care assessment. Spouses and civil partners are in law liable to support each other and can be asked to contribute towards fees, but the local authority should not do this if it would cause financial hardship. The local authority cannot ask an unmarried partner or other family member to contribute.

Planning ahead for care

If you think that you will need care for a long time, taking out a long-term care product could work out cheaper than the fees. Planning ahead is very difficult and there is no real way to know what your needs will be. There are a few providers of long-term care products and these tend to be expensive. One obvious route is to take out some form of insurance. In the UK, there is just one provider of long-term care insurance. It targets healthy individuals aged 50-70 years. With high premiums (for example around £100 per month for a policy that would pay out a flat rate of £1000 a month it is easy to see why the take up of this insurance is limited.

A handful of providers offer what is known as impaired life annuities that you buy at the point when you need care. You pay a lump sum and in return get an income that pays all or a substantial part of your care costs. The income is tax-free provided that it is paid direct to the provider. The amount that you pay for the annuity will depend on the monthly payments that you need and also the annuity providers assessment of how long that it will have to pay out.

19

Making a Will

It is often said that the toughest job in sales it to get people to buy fire extinguishers: no one wants to think that they and their family could be caught in a fire which could kill or injure. The same thinking seems to apply to making a will: most people in Britain have not made a will- something which their families could well come to regret.

There are two sorts of people for whom making a will is not just a good idea, but essential: Anyone who is reasonably well-off or whose affairs are at all complicated, and anyone who is in a partnership. Unmarried partners (or outside a civil arrangement) cannot inherit from each other unless there is a will: your partner could end up with nothing when you die, unless they can show that they were financially dependent.

There is no such thing in England as a 'common-law marriage.'

The State moves in

When anyone dies without making a will, the law, i.e. the state, takes over. In the extreme case, where you die single and have no other surviving relatives, all your estate could end up with the Crown. And the law is not at all generous to your spouse: if you have no children, your widow or widower is entitled to the first £200,000 of assets and 50% of what remains - the rest ending up with brothers and sisters, if you have any, or with relatives you cannot remember. If there are children, the widow/widower will get £125,000, plus personal assets and income from 50% of the rest; the children will get 50% when they reach age 18 and the other 50% when the surviving parents dies.

If you aim to save inheritance tax, you need to make a will. For 2009-10 the 'nil rate band' is fixed at £325,000 which means that no tax is due below that level, and anything more is taxed at 40%. How to save inheritance tax is discussed in the previous chapter but remember this: tax on the equivalent of the nil rate band is £130,000 - not chickenfeed!

How to make a will

So how do you make a will? You can draw up your own using a will-making kit which you can buy from a big stationer or download from the net. That represents the most cost-effective choice and it could work if your affairs are reasonably straightforward. But if you think that your will could be disputed, i.e. subject to legal challenge, then you need to go to a solicitor. That will be a few hundred pounds well spent and you may qualify for legal aid on financial grounds or because of age: you could ask citizens advice. You will probably know a solicitor or have employed one in a recent property deal. You will talk to friends or you can contact the Law Society for a list of solicitors near where you live.

Put yourself on paper

Before you go to your solicitor, there are two important things you need to do. Firstly, you need to put yourself on paper - everything you own that is of significant size, including cars, jewellery, property, home contents, bank accounts, shares and life insurance. At the same time, you put down all that you owe, such as mortgage, overdraft and credit card debts. You need to give precise details of the beneficiaries and be very specific about what you are leaving them.

The second thing you need to do is choose an executor, one or two people whose job is to ensure that your wishes are carried out. Your first thought may be someone younger than you (you will need their agreement to act) but there is no guarantee that they will outlive you. If no executor has been designated, the state will appoint a solicitor for you - for a fee. If you go to a solicitor, think about a formula, e.g. a partner appointed by whoever is senior partner of the firm at the time. The executors will need to know where your will is kept, with your solicitor or in your bank.

Time to revisit?

You have made your will, but you should resolve to look at it again, say every five years: people change, as do assets and liabilities. It is a good basic rule to revisit your will when a new child arrives or when you move house. Outside events can change a will: if you were single when you drew up your will, it may become invalid if you get married. But divorce or separation do not make a will invalid, so you might want to make changes. If you just want to make minor alterations, you can add supplementary changes known as codicils. These are added separately and all alterations have to be properly witnessed. If the alterations are significant, you will need to make a new will which will revoke any other wills you have made.

The case for making a will is essentially simple: as Benjamin Franklin said, death and taxes are certain, and making a will means that your family will not have to spend time and energy sorting out a complicated financial and legal set-up. But when you look beyond middle age you have to assess probabilities - you may be out of the country when your signature is needed, you may get ill or you may be injured. We are now talking power of attorney.

Power of attorney

You probably gave your solicitor a power of attorney when you sold your flat; you may have given a power of attorney to your partner when you had to go on an overseas business trip but wanted to buy some shares in the UK. A power of attorney simply gives a person the power to act for somebody else in their financial affairs or in health and personal welfare. (Rules in Scotland are different). The power of attorney you gave your solicitor was probably an ordinary power of attorney, created for a set period of time and for a specific piece of business. That all seems very practical, you may think, but why should you give anyone a power of attorney? The short answer is that if you are away or fall ill, you will need someone to look after your affairs - and that requires a power of attorney. (If this happens and you had not given a power of attorney, your friends and relatives would have to go to court, which would take time and cost money)

Ending the power

When you have given a power of attorney, there are two ways in which it can be ended. You can end it yourself by using a deed of revocation or it will end automatically if you, the donor, lose 'mental capacity.' This is where problems can arise. Suppose you gave your partner an ordinary power of attorney to handle your bank account while you go on your overseas business trip; you are mugged while on your trip and lie unconscious in hospital. Your power of attorney is ended because you are mentally out of action; for the same reason you cannot give a new power of attorney.

Your partner cannot legally access your bank account or have any involvement in your affairs: catch 22? Until last year, the answer to this puzzle was to create an Enduring Power of Attorney. Under an EPA when you were mugged on your overseas trip, your partner and/or solicitor would register with the court and they could then act on your behalf.

New EPAs cannot be created since October 2007 though any existing EPAs can be registered when that becomes necessary.

New lasting powers

EPA's have been replaced by Lasting Powers of Attorney which have separate sections for personal welfare and for property and affairs. Each of these has to be registered separately and the LP A can only be used - similar to an EPA - once it has been registered with the Office of the Public Guardian. If you want to change your mind, you can cancel all the different Powers of Attorney, so long as you are still mentally capable. This may all sound elaborate but it represents the only answer to the situation where you cannot manage your affairs because of accident, illness, age or whatever - but someone needs to do so.

The need for a power of attorney is now that much greater because banks and financial institutions are more aware of their legal responsibilities. Formerly, a friendly bank manager might have been prepared to help your partner sort out what needed to be done while you were out of action. Now, your friendly bank manager is more likely to stick to the legal rules, if only to protect himself and his employer.

You as attorney

One of your colleagues may ask you to be his attorney; if you agree, make sure that a firm of solicitors are also involved. You will have some costs - such as when you register the power of attorney - and there are strict rules, for keeping money and property separate and for keeping accounts of any dealings for the person who gave you the power. When you register, you are obliged to tell your colleague's relatives who are free to object. This is not a job for a layman acting all by himself

USEFUL ORGANISATIONS

MANAGEING MONEY

Association of Investment Trust Companies (AITC)
Durrant House
8-13 Chiswell Street
London EC1Y 4YY
Hotline: 0800 085 8520
www.aitc.co.uk

Debt Management Office
Eastcheap Court
11 Philpot Lane
London EC3M 8UD
Tel: 020 7862 6500
www.dmo.gov.uk

Department for Work and Pensions (DWP)
If you ring The Pension Service on 0845 606 0265,
You will be connected to the pension centre covering you area,
Or you can look on the website (www.
Thepensionservice.gov.uk/contact)

Another useful DWP website is www.pensionguide.gov.uk

You can obtain DWP leaflets from Pension Service and
Jobcentre Plus office and some post offices, CABs or
Libraries. You can write to:

Pension Guides
Freepost
Bristol BS38 7WA
Tel: 08457 31 32 33
If you have access to the Internet, you can download the leaflets
(and claim forms for many of the benefits)
from www.dwp.gov. uk or www.thepensionservice.gov.uk

Disability Alliance
Universal House
88-94 Wentworth Street
London E1 7SA
Tel: 020 7247 8776
www.disabilityalliance.org
Provides advice and publications on social security benefits
For disabled people.

Financial Ombudsman
Service (FOS)
South Quay Plaza
183 Marsh Wall
London E14 9SR
Consumer helpline: 0845 080 1800
www.financialombudsman.org.uk

Financial Services Authority (FSA)
25 The North Colonnade
Canary Wharf
London E14 5HS
Consumer helpline: 0845 606 1234
www.fsa.gov.uk/consummer

HM Revenue & Customs (HMRC)

The government department that deals
With al;most all the taxes due in the UK.
Most HMRC leaflets can be obtained
From local tax offices or Tax Enquiry Centres
(look for in the phone book under `Revenue'
or `Government Department')
or Jobcentre Plus offices.
Almost all are also available on the website at:
www.hmrc.gov.uk or you can ring them the Orderline:
Tel: 0845 900 0404   or write to :
PO Box 37
St Austel
Cornwall PL25 5YN

HM Revenue & Customs National Insurance

Contributions Office (NICO)
Benton Park View
Newcastle upon Tyne NE98 1ZZ
Enquiry Line: 0845 300 1479

International Pension Centre

The Pension Service
Tyneview Park
Newcastle upon Tyne NE98 1BA
Tel: 0191 7777
(8.00am-8.00pm,weekdays)

Investment Management Association

65 Kingsway
London WC2B 6TD
Tel: 020 7831 0898
Information line 020 7269 4639

www.investmentfunds.org.uk
(OEIC.S).

MoneyFACTS
MoneyFacts House
66-70 Thorpe Road
Norwich NR1 1BJ
Tel: 0870 2250 100
www.moneyfactsgroup.co.uk

Office of the Public Guardian
Archway Tower
2 Junction Road
 London N19 5SZ
Enquiry line: 0845 330 2900
Enduring Powers of Attorney: 0845 330 2963

The Pension Service
State Pension Forecasting Team
Future Pension Centre
Tyneview Park
Whitley Road Newcastle upon Tyne NE98 1BA
Tel: 0845 3000 168
www.thepensionservice.gove.uk

Pension Tracing Service
Tel: 0845 600 2537
www.thepensionservice.gov.uk

Pension Advisory Service
(TPAS)
11 Belgrave Road
London SW1V 1RB

Helpline: 0845 601 2923
www.pensionsadvisoryservice.org.uk

Principal Registry of the Family Division
(HM Courts Service)
First Avenue House
42-49 High Holborn
London WC1V 6NP
Tel: 020 7947 7000
www.courts-service.gov.uk
Wills can be lodged with the Probate Department ,
For a charge of £15. For information about
The leaflet `I want to deposit my will for safe
Keeping at the Principal Registry of the Family Division'.

Tax Help for Older People
Pineapple Business Park
Salway Ash
Bridport
Dorset DT6 5DB
Tel: 0845 601 3321
www.taxvol.org.uk

Department for Transport
Mobility and Inclusion Unit
Great Minster House
76 Marsham Street
London SW1P 4DR
Tel: 020 7944 8300
Blue Badge helpline: 020
7944 2914/0161 367 0009
www.dft.gov.uk

Disabled Persons Railcard
Office
PO Box 163
Newcastle upon Tyne
NE12 8WX
Tel:0845 605 0525
www.railcard.co.uk

Driver And Vehicle Licensing
Department (DVLA)
DVLA Driver Customer
Services
Swansea SA6 7JL
Driver enquiries: 0870 240
0009
www.dvla.gov.uk
DVLA Vehicle Customer
Services
Vehicle enquiries: 0870 240
0010
www.dvla.gov.uk

Mobility Information Services
(MIS)
20 Burton Close
Dawley
Telford TF4 2BX
Tel: 01743 340269
www.mis.org.uk

Mobility
Motability Car Scheme
City Gate House

22 Southwark Bridge Road
London SE1 9HB
Tel: 0845 456 4566
(8.30am- 5.30pm,weekdays)
www.motability.co.uk

Motability Wheelchair and Scooter Scheme
Route2mobility
Montgomery House
Newbury Road
Enham Alamein
Andover
Hampshire SP11 6JS

National Association of Councils for Voluntary And Community Service
(NACVS)
177 Arundel Street
Sheffield S1 2NU
Tel: 0114 278 6636
www.nacvs.org.uk

National Federation of Women's Institutes (NFWI)
104 New Kings Road
London SW6 4LY
Tel: 020 7371 9300
www.nfwi.org.uk

National Institute of Adult
Continuing Education

(NIACE)
Renaissance House
20 Princess Road West
Leicester LE1 6TP
Tel: 0116 204 4200/4201
www.niace.org.uk

Prime
Age Concern England
1268 London Road
London SW16 4ER
Helpline: 0800 783 1904
Tel: 020 8765 7833
www.primeinitiative.org.uk

RADAR (Royal Association For Disability and Rehabilitation)
12 City Forum
250 City Road
London EC1V 8AF
Tel: 020 7250 3222
www.radar.org.uk

REACH
89 Albert Embankment
London SE1 7TP
Tel: 020 7582 6543
www.reach-online.org.uk

Retired and Senior Volunteer
Programme (RSVP)
237 Pentonville Road
London N1 9NJ

Tel: 020 7643 1385
www.csv-rsvp.org.uk

The Age Employment

Network (TAEN)
207-221 Pentonville Road
London N1 9UZ
Tel: 020 7843 1590
www.taen.org.uk

RUNNING YOUR HOME

Abbeyfield Society

Abbeyfield House
53 Victoria Street
St Albans
Hertfordshire AL1 3UW
Tel: 01727 857536
www.abbeyfield.com

AIMS (Advice Information and Mediation Service for Retirement housing)

Astral House
1268 London Road
London SW16 4ER
Advice line: 0845 600 2001
www.ageconcern.org.uk/aims

Almshouse Association

Billingbear Lodge
Maidenhead Road
Wokingham

Berkshire RG40 5RU
Tel: 01344 452922
www.almshouses.org

Department for Environment, Food and Rural Affairs

(DEFRA)
Pet Travel Scheme(PETS)
Eastbury House
30 –34 Albert Embankment
London SE1 7TL
Helpline: 08459 33 55 77
www.defra.gov.uk/animalh/quarantine

Disabled Living Foundation

(DLF)
380-384 Harrow Road
London W9 2HU
Helpline: 0845 130 9177
Demonstration centre:
0845 130 9177
Tel: 020 7289 6111
www.dlf.org.uk

Eaga Partnership Charitable Trust (eaga plc)

Eage House
Archbold Terrace
Newcastle upon Tyne NE2
1DB
Tel: 01768 210 220
www.eaga.co.uk

**Elderly Accommodation
Counsel (EAC)**
3rd Floor
89 Albert Embankment
London SE1 7TP
Adviceline: 020 7820 1343
www.housingcare.org

Energywatch
Percy House
Percy Street
Newcastle upon Tyne NE1
4PW
Helpline: 0845 906 0708
www.energywatch.org.uk

**Federation of Master
Builders (FMB)**
Gordon Fisher House
14-15 Great James Street
London WC1N 3DP
Tel: 020 7242 7583
www.fmb.org.uk

**Foundations (the national co-ordinating
Body for home improvement agencies)**
Bleaklow House
Howard Town Mill
Glossop SK13 8HT
Tel: 01457 891909
www.foundations.uk.com

Home Improvement Trust
7 Mansfield Road
Nottingham NG1 3FB
Tel: 0800 783 7569
www.hitrust.org

National House Building
Council (NHBC)
NHBC House
Davy Avenue
Knowlhill
Milton Keynes MK5 8FP
Tel: 0844 633 100
www.nhbc.co.uk

Trust Mark
Englemere
Kings Ride
Ascot SL5 7TB
Tel:0870 163 7373
www.trustmark.org.uk

STAYING HEALTHY

Ageing Well UK
Age Concern England
1268 London Road
London SW16 4ER
Information line:0800 00 99 66
www. Ageconcern.org.uk/
AgeConcern/ageingwell

Arthritis Care

18 Stephenson Way
London NW1 2HD
Helpline: 0808 800 4050
Tel: 020 7380 6500
www.athritiscare.org.uk

Breast Cancer Care

210 New Kings Road
London SW6 4NZ
Helpline:0808 800 6000
www.breastcancercare.org.ul

British Dental Health

Foundation
Smile House
2 East Union Street
Rugby
Warwickshire CV22 6AJ
Helpline: 0845 063 1188
Tel: 0870 770 4000
www.dentalhealth.org.uk

British Heart Foundation

14 Fitzhardinge Street
London W1H 6DH
Information line: 0845 070 8070
Tel: 020 7935 0185
www.bhf.org.uk

Cancerbackup

3 Bath Place
Rivingtin Street

London EC2A 3JR
Helpline: 0808 800 1234
(9am-8pm, weekdays)
Textphone: 18001 0808 800 1234
www.cancerbackup.org.uk

Diabetes UK
Macleod House
10 Parkway
London NW1 7AA
Careline: 0845 120 2960
Tel: 020 7424 1000
www.diabetes.org.uk

Hearing Concern
95 Gray's Inn Road
London WC1X 8TX
HelpDesk: 0845 0744 600
(voice & text)
Tel: 020 7440 9871
Textphone:020 7440 9873 {?1}
www.hearingconcern.org.uk

Incontact
SATRA Innovation Park
Rockingham Road
Kettering NN16 9JH
Helpline:0845 345 0165
www.incontact.org

Institute of Trichologists
Ground Floor Office
24 Langroyd Road

London SW17 7PL
Tel: 0870 607 0602
www.trichologists.org.uk

Keep Fit Association
1 Grove House
Foundry Lane
Horsham
West Sussex RH13 5PL
Tel: 01493 266000
www.keepfit.org.uk

National Osteoporosis Society (NOS)
Manor Farm
Skinners Hill Camerton Bath BA2 OPJ
Tel: 01761 471771
Helpline: 0845 450 0230
www.nos.org.uk

NHS DIRECT
Tel:0845 46 47
Nhsdirect.nhs.uk
24- hour telephone and on line advice

NHS Drinkline
Freephone: 0800 917 8282
(9.00am- 11.00pm, weekdays)

Patients Association
PO Box 935
Harrow
Middlesex HA1 3YJ

Helpline: 0845 608 4455
Tel: 020 8423 9111
www.patientsassociation.com

Royal National Institute of BLIND People (RNIB)

105 Judd Street
London WC1H 9NE
Helpline: 0845 766 9999
Tel: 020 7388 1266
www.rnib.org.uk

Royal National Institute for Deaf People (RNID)

19-23 Featherstone Street
London EC1Y 8SL
Information Line: 0808 808 0123
Textphone Helpline:0808 808 9000
www.rnid.org.uk

Crossroads Caring for Carers

10 Regent Place
Rugby CV21 2PN
Helpline: 0845 450 0350
www.crossroads.org.uk

Cruse-Bereavement Care

PO Box 800
Richmond
Surrey TW9 1RG
Helpline: 0870 167 1677
Tel: 020 8939 9530
www.crusebereavementcare.org.uk

Family Rights Group
2nd Floor
The Print House
18 Ashwin Street
London E8 3DL
Advice Line: 0800 7311 696
Tel: 020 7923 2628
www.frg.org.uk

Grandparents' Association
Moot House
The Stow
Harlow
Essex CM20 3AG
Helpline: 0845 4349 585
Tel: 0279 428040
www.grandparentsassociation.org.uk

Grandparents Plus
18 Victoria Park Square
London E2 9PF
Tel: 020 8981 8001
www.grandparentsplus.org.uk

Relate
Premier House
Caroline Court
Lakeside
Doncaster DN4 5RA
Tel: 0300 100 1234
www.relate.org.uk

**United Kingdom Home
Care Association (UKHCA)**
2nd Floor
Group House
52 Sutton Court Road
Sutton
Surrey SM1 4SL
Tel: 020 8288 5291
www.ukhca.co.uk

**WRVS (Women's Royal
Voluntary Service)**
Garden House
Milton Hill
Abingdon OX13 6AD
Tel: 01235 442900
www.wrvs.org.uk

Index

www.straightforwardco.co.uk

All titles, listed below, in the Straightforward Guides Series can be purchased online, using credit card or other forms of payment by going to www.straightfowardco.co.uk A discount of 25% per title is offered with online purchases.

Law

A Straightforward Guide to:

Consumer Rights

Bankruptcy Insolvency and the Law

Employment Law

Private Tenants Rights

Family law

Small Claims in the County Court

Contract law

Intellectual Property and the law

Divorce and the law

Leaseholders Rights

The Process of Conveyancing

Knowing Your Rights and Using the Courts

Producing Your own Will

Housing Rights

The Bailiff the law and You

Probate and The Law

Company law

What to Expect When You Go to Court

Guide to Competition Law

Give me Your Money-Guide to Effective Debt Collection

Caring for a Disabled Child

General titles
Letting Property for Profit
Buying, Selling and Renting property
Buying a Home in England and France
Bookkeeping and Accounts for Small Business
Creative Writing
Freelance Writing
Writing Your own Life Story
Writing performance Poetry
Writing Romantic Fiction
Speech Writing
Teaching Your Child to Read and write
Teaching Your Child to Swim
Raising a Child-The Early Years
Creating a Successful Commercial Website
The Straightforward Business Plan
The Straightforward C.V.
Successful Public Speaking
Handling Bereavement
Play the Game-A Compendium of Rules
Individual and Personal Finance
Understanding Mental Illness
The Two Minute Message
Guide to Self Defence
Buying a Used Car
Tiling for Beginners

Go to:

www.straightforwardco.co.uk